Ways into Science

Where Things Live

Written by Peter Riley

W
FRANKLIN WATTS
LONDON•SYDNEY

First published in 2003 by Franklin Watts
96 Leonard Street, London EC2A 4XD

Franklin Watts Australia
45-51 Huntley Street
Alexandria, NSW 2015

Series editor: Sarah Peutrill
Art director: Jonathan Hair
Design: Ian Thompson
Photography: Ray Moller (unless otherwise credited)

A CIP catalogue record for this book is available from
the British Library

ISBN 0 7496 4736 1

Printed in Hong Kong/China

Picture Credits:
L. Batten/FLPA p. 18b; Granville Harris/Bruce Coleman
Collection p. 6c; Sally Morgan/Ecoscene p. 13br; Robert
Pickett/Papilio pp. 13cl, 22cr, 22bl, 22br; Ken Preston-
Mafham/Premaphotos Wildlife pp. 9t, 10br, 15cr, 15bl, 15br,
17b, 20tl, 20cl, 20cr; Dr. Rod Preston-Mafham/Premaphotos
Wildlife p. 9c; C. Mattison/FLPA p. 6b; Hans Reinhard/Bruce
Coleman Collection pp. 20br, 22cl; Ken Sperrin/Papilio p. 21c;
Colin Varndell/Bruce Coleman Collection p. 16tl; Barrie Watts
cover & pp. 10bl, 12cr, 15cl

Thanks to our models:
Amber Barkhouse, Reece Calvert, Shani-e Cox,
Chantelle Daniel, Ammar Duffus, Alex Green,
Harry Johal and Emily Scott

To my granddaughter Megan Kate

Contents

Where do plants and animals live?

Plants and animals live in all sorts of places.

Some plants and animals live in grassy places like this field.

Some live in stony places.

This pond is full of living things.

Trees are home to living things as well.

Different living things like to live in different places.

A grassy place

Lots of plants live in a grassy place like this lawn.

Clover

Daisy

Dandelion

Look at a lawn. Can you see the plants shown here?

Some animals live in grassy places, too.

Ground beetles live in damp grass.

A harvestman lives in tall grass. It has eight long thin legs like a spider.

Look closely at a lawn. Can you see any animals?

Life in the soil

Sam has dug up some soil. He puts it on a white tray and spreads it out.

This is what he finds.

Earthworms

Grub

The grub will become a beetle or fly.

Laura puts some soil and
earthworms in a plastic bottle.

She puts some
leaves on the top.

She puts paper
around the bottle
to make it dark.

What happens in the soil
after a few days?
Turn the page to find out.

tunnels

The earthworms made tunnels in the soil. Earthworms find food in the soil as they eat their way through it.

Try making a home for worms.

Plants and soil

Plants grow their roots in soil.

Sea holly
likes to grow
in sandy soils.

Marsh plants
like to grow in
very wet soil.

Stony places

Sometimes there is soil in the cracks between stones.

Some plants can grow there.

Can you find plants in cracks between stones?

Some animals live under stones.

You can see them by carefully turning over the stone.

Here are some of the animals you may find.

Slug

Centipede

Ground beetle

Woodlice

Remember to turn the stones back again.

Under a tree

Some trees lose their leaves in the autumn.

The fallen leaves are called leaf litter.

Leaf litter is a home for some animals.

Hannah collects some leaf litter.

She empties the bag onto a white sheet.

She moves the leaves apart.

Hannah finds some millipedes.

She puts the leaves and animals back where she found them.

Try finding animals in leaf litter.

On a tree

A tree is a plant. Some other plants can live on trees.

Moss plants live on damp bark.

Ivy plants grow on tree trunks.

Raj wants to see what animals are living on a branch.

He puts a white sheet under a branch.

He shakes the branch.

What does Raj see? Turn the page to find out.

On a branch

Spider

Raj sees spiders, aphids, weevils and caterpillars.

Weevil

Aphids

Raj empties the sheet close to the tree so the animals can go back to it.

Caterpillar

Try this test. What do you find?

 Pond life

Lots of animals and plants live
in or around a pond.

What animals do you think you
might find in this pond?

Make a list and then turn
the page to find out.

Pond creatures

Here are some animals
that live in a pond.

Fish

Pond snail

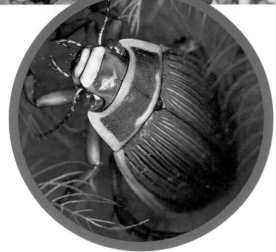

Water beetle

22

Tadpole

Matthew is making a home for pond snails.

He puts gravel in the bottom of a tank.

He puts water plants in the gravel.

He pours in some water and puts in the snails.

Make a home for pond snails.
Look at them every day.
What do you find out?

Woodlice home

Here are some woodlice. Katie is making a home for them.

She puts soil in the bottom of a tank.

She puts leaves, grass, moss, stones and wood on top of the soil.

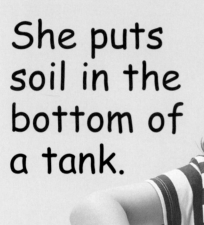

Katie puts the woodlice in the tank.

She leaves it for an hour then looks to see where the woodlice are.

They are under the stones and wood.

Try Katie's test to see where your woodlice go.

After the test remember to set the woodlice free where you found them.

Making a survey

Paul is doing a survey about animals living under stones.

He turns over five stones and looks at the animals living under them.

He records his results in a table.

Animal	Stone					Total
	1	2	3	4	5	
Woodlouse						
Earthworm						
Beetle						
Spider						
Snail						
Millipede						

Try this survey yourself.

Nicole is doing a survey about plants.

She throws a hoop to five different places on a lawn.

She records the plants she sees inside the hoop each time.

Plant	Hoop					Total
	1	2	3	4	5	
Grass						
Buttercup						
Daisy						
Dandelion						
Thistle						
Moss						

Try this survey yourself.

Useful words

aphid – a small insect that eats plants.

autumn – the season of the year after summer when the weather gets cooler, wetter and windier.

bark – a cover on the trunk, branches and twigs of trees and bushes.

branch – a side shoot from the trunks of trees or bushes.

field – a large area of grass with a fence, walls or hedges round it.

gravel – small stones used in aquarium tanks to hold water plants in place.

grub – the young stage of a beetle or some kinds of fly.

lawn – an area of ground covered in short grass.

millipede – a long thin animal with a large number of legs.

pond – a hole that is filled with water all year round.

roots – the parts of a plant in the soil. They take up water from the soil and hold the plant in place.

sea holly – a plant that grows in sandy soil near the sea.

soil – a mixture of tiny pieces of rock and tiny pieces of dead plants and animals.

Some answers

Here are some answers to the questions we have asked in this book. Don't worry if you had some different answers to ours; you may be right, too. Talk through your answers with other people and see if you can explain why they are right.

Page 8 Most lawns do not just have grass in them. There may be daisies, dandelions and clover. You may also find buttercups and moss in some lawns.

Page 9 Spiders may be seen running under the grass. Occasionally a beetle may be seen on top of the grass. Harvestmen may be seen in shady corners of a lawn. Sometimes crane-flies (daddy-long-legs) can be seen resting on a lawn.

Page 14 Plants can be found growing in cracks in the pavement and between the stones on a wall.

Page 20 The number and type of animals will depend on the plant and the position of the branch. Try a branch on a sunny side and one on a shady side of the tree. Aphids should be found on most branches. Spiders and caterpillars are found frequently. Weevils may be found occasionally.

Page 23 The snails may glide over the side of the tank and lick off green algae.

Page 25 Woodlice will be found in the darkest and dampest places.

Index

About this book

Ways into Science is designed to encourage children to begin to think about their everyday world in a scientific way, examining cause and effect through close observation, recording their results and discussing what they have seen. Here are some pointers to gain maximum use from **Where Things Live**.

• Working through this book will introduce the basic concepts about where things live and also some of the associated vocabulary.

• On pages 11, 19 and 21 the children are invited to predict the results of a particular action or test. Ensure that you discuss the reason for any answer they give in some depth before turning over the page. In answering the question on page 11 look for an answer about mixing up the soil. In answering the question on page 19 look for an answer about 'creepy crawlies' falling off the branch. In answering the question on page 21 the children may mention fish and frogs. They may also mention ducks.

• Making a survey as on pages 26 and 27 is a useful practical activity in finding out about the distribution of living things. This introduces the tasks of recording data in a table, performing a simple calculation (addition), making comparisons and drawing conclusions. When looking under stones woodlice and beetles may be found most frequently, but in damp areas earthworms and snails may predominate. If a centipede is encountered it will run away quickly. The plant survey will depend on the lawn but moss may be found in damp areas while daisies and dandelions may be found scattered over the whole area. Thistles are likely to be the least numerous. The children should close their eyes as they throw the hoops so that the area for sampling is selected at random.